ELIZABETH II

Unfair Contract Terms Act 1977

1977 CHAPTER 50

An Act to impose further limits on the extent to which under the law of England and Wales and Northern Ireland civil liability for breach of contract, or for negligence or other breach of duty, can be avoided by means of contract terms and otherwise, and under the law of Scotland civil liability can be avoided by means of contract terms. [26th October 1977]

BE IT ENACTED by the Queen's most Excellent Majesty, by and with the advice and consent of the Lords Spiritual and Temporal, and Commons, in this present Parliament assembled, and by the authority of the same, as follows:—

PART I

AMENDMENT OF LAW FOR ENGLAND AND WALES AND NORTHERN IRELAND

Introductory

1.—(1) For the purposes of this Part of this Act, " negligence " means the breach— *Scope of Part I.*

    (a) of any obligation, arising from the express or implied terms of a contract, to take reasonable care or exercise reasonable skill in the performance of the contract;

    (b) of any common law duty to take reasonable care or exercise reasonable skill (but not any stricter duty);

PART I
1957 c. 31.
1957 c. 25 (N.I.).

    (c) of the common duty of care imposed by the Occupiers' Liability Act 1957 or the Occupiers' Liability Act (Northern Ireland) 1957.

(2) This Part of this Act is subject to Part III; and in relation to contracts, the operation of sections 2 to 4 and 7 is subject to the exceptions made by Schedule 1.

(3) In the case of both contract and tort, sections 2 to 7 apply (except where the contrary is stated in section 6(4)) only to business liability, that is liability for breach of obligations or duties arising—

    (a) from things done or to be done by a person in the course of a business (whether his own business or another's); or

    (b) from the occupation of premises used for business purposes of the occupier;

and references to liability are to be read accordingly.

(4) In relation to any breach of duty or obligation, it is immaterial for any purpose of this Part of this Act whether the breach was inadvertent or intentional, or whether liability for it arises directly or vicariously.

Avoidance of liability for negligence, breach of contract, etc.

Negligence liability.

2.—(1) A person cannot by reference to any contract term or to a notice given to persons generally or to particular persons exclude or restrict his liability for death or personal injury resulting from negligence.

(2) In the case of other loss or damage, a person cannot so exclude or restrict his liability for negligence except in so far as the term or notice satisfies the requirement of reasonableness.

(3) Where a contract term or notice purports to exclude or restrict liability for negligence a person's agreement to or awareness of it is not of itself to be taken as indicating his voluntary acceptance of any risk.

Liability arising in contract.

3.—(1) This section applies as between contracting parties where one of them deals as consumer or on the other's written standard terms of business.

(2) As against that party, the other cannot by reference to any contract term—

    (a) when himself in breach of contract, exclude or restrict any liability of his in respect of the breach; or

    (b) claim to be entitled—

        (i) to render a contractual performance substantially different from that which was reasonably expected of him, or

PART I

(ii) in respect of the whole or any part of his contractual obligation, to render no performance at all,

except in so far as (in any of the cases mentioned above in this subsection) the contract term satisfies the requirement of reasonableness.

Unreasonable indemnity clauses.

4.—(1) A person dealing as consumer cannot by reference to any contract term be made to indemnify another person (whether a party to the contract or not) in respect of liability that may be incurred by the other for negligence or breach of contract, except in so far as the contract term satisfies the requirement of reasonableness.

(2) This section applies whether the liability in question—
   (*a*) is directly that of the person to be indemnified or is incurred by him vicariously;
   (*b*) is to the person dealing as consumer or to someone else.

Liability arising from sale or supply of goods

"Guarantee" of consumer goods.

5.—(1) In the case of goods of a type ordinarily supplied for private use or consumption, where loss or damage—
   (*a*) arises from the goods proving defective while in consumer use; and
   (*b*) results from the negligence of a person concerned in the manufacture or distribution of the goods,

liability for the loss or damage cannot be excluded or restricted by reference to any contract term or notice contained in or operating by reference to a guarantee of the goods.

(2) For these purposes—
   (*a*) goods are to be regarded as "in consumer use" when a person is using them, or has them in his possession for use, otherwise than exclusively for the purposes of a business; and
   (*b*) anything in writing is a guarantee if it contains or purports to contain some promise or assurance (however worded or presented) that defects will be made good by complete or partial replacement, or by repair, monetary compensation or otherwise.

(3) This section does not apply as between the parties to a contract under or in pursuance of which possession or ownership of the goods passed.

Sale and hire-purchase. 56 & 57 Vict. c. 71.

6.—(1) Liability for breach of the obligations arising from—
   (*a*) section 12 of the Sale of Goods Act 1893 (seller's implied undertakings as to title, etc.);

PART I
1973 c. 13.

(b) section 8 of the Supply of Goods (Implied Terms) Act 1973 (the corresponding thing in relation to hire-purchase),

cannot be excluded or restricted by reference to any contract term.

(2) As against a person dealing as consumer, liability for breach of the obligations arising from—

(a) section 13, 14 or 15 of the 1893 Act (seller's implied undertakings as to conformity of goods with description or sample, or as to their quality or fitness for a particular purpose);

(b) section 9, 10 or 11 of the 1973 Act (the corresponding things in relation to hire-purchase),

cannot be excluded or restricted by reference to any contract term.

(3) As against a person dealing otherwise than as consumer, the liability specified in subsection (2) above can be excluded or restricted by reference to a contract term, but only in so far as the term satisfies the requirement of reasonableness.

(4) The liabilities referred to in this section are not only the business liabilities defined by section 1(3), but include those arising under any contract of sale of goods or hire-purchase agreement.

Miscellaneous contracts under which goods pass.

7.—(1) Where the possession or ownership of goods passes under or in pursuance of a contract not governed by the law of sale of goods or hire-purchase, subsections (2) to (4) below apply as regards the effect (if any) to be given to contract terms excluding or restricting liability for breach of obligation arising by implication of law from the nature of the contract.

(2) As against a person dealing as consumer, liability in respect of the goods' correspondence with description or sample, or their quality or fitness for any particular purpose, cannot be excluded or restricted by reference to any such term.

(3) As against a person dealing otherwise than as consumer, that liability can be excluded or restricted by reference to such a term, but only in so far as the term satisfies the requirement of reasonableness.

(4) Liability in respect of—

(a) the right to transfer ownership of the goods, or give possession; or

(b) the assurance of quiet possession to a person taking goods in pursuance of the contract, cannot be excluded or restricted by reference to any such term except in so far as the term satisfies the requirement of reasonableness.

(5) This section does not apply in the case of goods passing on a redemption of trading stamps within the Trading Stamps Act 1964 or the Trading Stamps Act (Northern Ireland) 1965.

1964 c. 71.
1965 c. 6.
(N.I.).

Other provisions about contracts

8.—(1) In the Misrepresentation Act 1967, the following is substituted for section 3—

Misrepresentation.
1967 c. 7.

"Avoidance of provision excluding liability for misrepresentation.

3. If a contract contains a term which would exclude or restrict—

(a) any liability to which a party to a contract may be subject by reason of any misrepresentation made by him before the contract was made ; or

(b) any remedy available to another party to the contract by reason of such a misrepresentation,

that term shall be of no effect except in so far as it satisfies the requirement of reasonableness as stated in section 11(1) of the Unfair Contract Terms Act 1977 ; and it is for those claiming that the term satisfies that requirement to show that it does.".

(2) The same section is substituted for section 3 of the Misrepresentation Act (Northern Ireland) 1967.

1967 c. 14
(N.I.).

9.—(1) Where for reliance upon it a contract term has to satisfy the requirement of reasonableness, it may be found to do so and be given effect accordingly notwithstanding that the contract has been terminated either by breach or by a party electing to treat it as repudiated.

Effect of breach.

(2) Where on a breach the contract is nevertheless affirmed by a party entitled to treat it as repudiated, this does not of itself exclude the requirement of reasonableness in relation to any contract term.

10. A person is not bound by any contract term prejudicing or taking away rights of his which arise under, or in connection with the performance of, another contract, so far as those rights extend to the enforcement of another's liability which this Part of this Act prevents that other from excluding or restricting.

Evasion by means of secondary contract.

PART I

The "reasonableness" test.
1967 c. 7.
1967 c. 14. (N.I.).

"Dealing as consumer".

Explanatory provisions

11.—(1) In relation to a contract term, the requirement of reasonableness for the purposes of this Part of this Act, section 3 of the Misrepresentation Act 1967 and section 3 of the Misrepresentation Act (Northern Ireland) 1967 is that the term shall have been a fair and reasonable one to be included having regard to the circumstances which were, or ought reasonably to have been, known to or in the contemplation of the parties when the contract was made.

(2) In determining for the purposes of section 6 or 7 above whether a contract term satisfies the requirement of reasonableness, regard shall be had in particular to the matters specified in Schedule 2 to this Act; but this subsection does not prevent the court or arbitrator from holding, in accordance with any rule of law, that a term which purports to exclude or restrict any relevant liability is not a term of the contract.

(3) In relation to a notice (not being a notice having contractual effect), the requirement of reasonableness under this Act is that it should be fair and reasonable to allow reliance on it, having regard to all the circumstances obtaining when the liability arose or (but for the notice) would have arisen.

(4) Where by reference to a contract term or notice a person seeks to restrict liability to a specified sum of money, and the question arises (under this or any other Act) whether the term or notice satisfies the requirement of reasonableness, regard shall be had in particular (but without prejudice to subsection (2) above in the case of contract terms) to—

(*a*) the resources which he could expect to be available to him for the purpose of meeting the liability should it arise; and

(*b*) how far it was open to him to cover himself by insurance.

(5) It is for those claiming that a contract term or notice satisfies the requirement of reasonableness to show that it does.

12.—(1) A party to a contract " deals as consumer " in relation to another party if—

(*a*) he neither makes the contract in the course of a business nor holds himself out as doing so; and

(*b*) the other party does make the contract in the course of a business; and

(c) in the case of a contract governed by the law of sale of goods or hire-purchase, or by section 7 of this Act, the goods passing under or in pursuance of the contract are of a type ordinarily supplied for private use or consumption.

(2) But on a sale by auction or by competitive tender the buyer is not in any circumstances to be regarded as dealing as consumer.

(3) Subject to this, it is for those claiming that a party does not deal as consumer to show that he does not.

13.—(1) To the extent that this Part of this Act prevents the exclusion or restriction of any liability it also prevents—

(a) making the liability or its enforcement subject to restrictive or onerous conditions;

(b) excluding or restricting any right or remedy in respect of the liability, or subjecting a person to any prejudice in consequence of his pursuing any such right or remedy;

(c) excluding or restricting rules of evidence or procedure;

and (to that extent) sections 2 and 5 to 7 also prevent excluding or restricting liability by reference to terms and notices which exclude or restrict the relevant obligation or duty.

(2) But an agreement in writing to submit present or future differences to arbitration is not to be treated under this Part of this Act as excluding or restricting any liability.

14. In this Part of this Act—

"business" includes a profession and the activities of any government department or local or public authority;

"goods" has the same meaning as in the Sale of Goods Act 1893;

"hire-purchase agreement" has the same meaning as in the Consumer Credit Act 1974;

"negligence" has the meaning given by section 1(1);

"notice" includes an announcement, whether or not in writing, and any other communication or pretended communication; and

"personal injury" includes any disease and any impairment of physical or mental condition.

PART II

AMENDMENT OF LAW FOR SCOTLAND

Scope of Part II.

15.—(1) This Part of this Act applies only to contracts, is subject to Part III of this Act and does not affect the validity of any discharge or indemnity given by a person in consideration of the receipt by him of compensation in settlement of any claim which he has.

(2) Subject to subsection (3) below, sections 16 to 18 of this Act apply to any contract only to the extent that the contract—

(a) relates to the transfer of the ownership or possession of goods from one person to another (with or without work having been done on them);

(b) constitutes a contract of service or apprenticeship;

(c) relates to services of whatever kind, including (without prejudice to the foregoing generality) carriage, deposit and pledge, care and custody, mandate, agency, loan and services relating to the use of land;

(d) relates to the liability of an occupier of land to persons entering upon or using that land;

(e) relates to a grant of any right or permission to enter upon or use land not amounting to an estate or interest in the land.

(3) Notwithstanding anything in subsection (2) above, sections 16 to 18—

(a) do not apply to any contract to the extent that the contract—

(i) is a contract of insurance (including a contract to pay an annuity on human life);

(ii) relates to the formation, constitution or dissolution of any body corporate or unincorporated association or partnership;

(b) apply to—

a contract of marine salvage or towage;

a charter party of a ship or hovercraft;

a contract for the carriage of goods by ship or hovercraft; or,

a contract to which subsection (4) below relates,

only to the extent that—

(i) both parties deal or hold themselves out as dealing in the course of a business (and then only in so far as the contract purports to exclude or restrict liability for breach of duty in respect of death or personal injury); or

(ii) the contract is a consumer contract (and then only in favour of the consumer).

(4) This subsection relates to a contract in pursuance of which goods are carried by ship or hovercraft and which either—

   (a) specifies ship or hovercraft as the means of carriage over part of the journey to be covered; or

   (b) makes no provision as to the means of carriage and does not exclude ship or hovercraft as that means,

in so far as the contract operates for and in relation to the carriage of the goods by that means.

16.—(1) Where a term of a contract purports to exclude or restrict liability for breach of duty arising in the course of any business or from the occupation of any premises used for business purposes of the occupier, that term—

   (a) shall be void in any case where such exclusion or restriction is in respect of death or personal injury;

   (b) shall, in any other case, have no effect if it was not fair and reasonable to incorporate the term in the contract.

Liability for breach of duty.

(2) Subsection (1)(a) above does not affect the validity of any discharge and indemnity given by a person, on or in connection with an award to him of compensation for pneumoconiosis attributable to employment in the coal industry, in respect of any further claim arising from his contracting that disease.

(3) Where under subsection (1) above a term of a contract is void or has no effect, the fact that a person agreed to, or was aware of, the term shall not of itself be sufficient evidence that he knowingly and voluntarily assumed any risk.

17.—(1) Any term of a contract which is a consumer contract or a standard form contract shall have no effect for the purpose of enabling a party to the contract—

   (a) who is in breach of a contractual obligation, to exclude or restrict any liability of his to the consumer or customer in respect of the breach;

   (b) in respect of a contractual obligation, to render no performance, or to render a performance substantially different from that which the consumer or customer reasonably expected from the contract;

if it was not fair and reasonable to incorporate the term in the contract.

Control of unreasonable exemptions in consumer or standard form contracts.

(2) In this section "customer" means a party to a standard form contract who deals on the basis of written standard terms of business of the other party to the contract who himself deals in the course of a business.

PART II
Unreasonable indemnity clauses in consumer contracts.

18.—(1) Any term of a contract which is a consumer contract shall have no effect for the purpose of making the consumer indemnify another person (whether a party to the contract or not) in respect of liability which that other person may incur as a result of breach of duty or breach of contract, if it was not fair and reasonable to incorporate the term in the contract.

(2) In this section " liability " means liability arising in the course of any business or from the occupation of any premises used for business purposes of the occupier.

" Guarantee " of consumer goods.

19.—(1) This section applies to a guarantee—
  (a) in relation to goods which are of a type ordinarily supplied for private use or consumption ; and
  (b) which is not a guarantee given by one party to the other party to a contract under or in pursuance of which the ownership or possession of the goods to which the guarantee relates is transferred.

(2) A term of a guarantee to which this section applies shall be void in so far as it purports to exclude or restrict liability for loss or damage (including death or personal injury)—
  (a) arising from the goods proving defective while—
    (i) in use otherwise than exclusively for the purposes of a business ; or
    (ii) in the possession of a person for such use ; and
  (b) resulting from the breach of duty of a person concerned in the manufacture or distribution of the goods.

(3) For the purposes of this section, any document is a guarantee if it contains or purports to contain some promise or assurance (however worded or presented) that defects will be made good by complete or partial replacement, or by repair, monetary compensation or otherwise.

Obligations implied by law in sale and hire-purchase contracts.
56 & 57 Vict. c. 71.
1973 c. 13.

20.—(1) Any term of a contract which purports to exclude or restrict liability for breach of the obligations arising from—
  (a) section 12 of the Sale of Goods Act 1893 (seller's implied undertakings as to title etc.) ;
  (b) section 8 of the Supply of Goods (Implied Terms) Act 1973 (implied terms as to title in hire-purchase agreements),
shall be void.

PART II

(2) Any term of a contract which purports to exclude or restrict liability for breach of the obligations arising from—
  (a) section 13, 14 or 15 of the said Act of 1893 (seller's implied undertakings as to conformity of goods with description or sample, or as to their quality or fitness for a particular purpose);
  (b) section 9, 10 or 11 of the said Act of 1973 (the corresponding provisions in relation to hire-purchase),
shall—
    (i) in the case of a consumer contract, be void against the consumer;
    (ii) in any other case, have no effect if it was not fair and reasonable to incorporate the term in the contract.

Obligations implied by law in other contracts for the supply of goods.

21.—(1) Any term of a contract to which this section applies purporting to exclude or restrict liability for breach of an obligation—
  (a) such as is referred to in subsection (3)(a) below—
    (i) in the case of a consumer contract, shall be void against the consumer, and
    (ii) in any other case, shall have no effect if it was not fair and reasonable to incorporate the term in the contract;
  (b) such as is referred to in subsection (3)(b) below, shall have no effect if it was not fair and reasonable to incorporate the term in the contract.

(2) This section applies to any contract to the extent that it relates to any such matter as is referred to in section 15(2)(a) of this Act, but does not apply to—
  (a) a contract of sale of goods or a hire-purchase agreement; or
  (b) a charterparty of a ship or hovercraft unless it is a consumer contract (and then only in favour of the consumer).

(3) An obligation referred to in this subsection is an obligation incurred under a contract in the course of a business and arising by implication of law from the nature of the contract which relates—
  (a) to the correspondence of goods with description or sample, or to the quality or fitness of goods for any particular purpose; or
  (b) to any right to transfer ownership or possession of goods, or to the enjoyment of quiet possession of goods.

(4) Nothing in this section applies to the supply of goods on a redemption of trading stamps within the Trading Stamps Act 1964.

1964 c. 71.

PART II
Consequence of breach.

22. For the avoidance of doubt, where any provision of this Part of this Act requires that the incorporation of a term in a contract must be fair and reasonable for that term to have effect—
  (a) if that requirement is satisfied, the term may be given effect to notwithstanding that the contract has been terminated in consequence of breach of that contract;
  (b) for the term to be given effect to, that requirement must be satisfied even where a party who is entitled to rescind the contract elects not to rescind it.

Evasion by means of secondary contract.

23. Any term of any contract shall be void which purports to exclude or restrict, or has the effect of excluding or restricting—
  (a) the exercise, by a party to any other contract, of any right or remedy which arises in respect of that other contract in consequence of breach of duty, or of obligation, liability for which could not by virtue of the provisions of this Part of this Act be excluded or restricted by a term of that other contract;
  (b) the application of the provisions of this Part of this Act in respect of that or any other contract.

The "reasonableness" test.

24.—(1) In determining for the purposes of this Part of this Act whether it was fair and reasonable to incorporate a term in a contract, regard shall be had only to the circumstances which were, or ought reasonably to have been, known to or in the contemplation of the parties to the contract at the time the contract was made.

(2) In determining for the purposes of section 20 or 21 of this Act whether it was fair and reasonable to incorporate a term in a contract, regard shall be had in particular to the matters specified in Schedule 2 to this Act; but this subsection shall not prevent a court or arbiter from holding, in accordance with any rule of law, that a term which purports to exclude or restrict any relevant liability is not a term of the contract.

(3) Where a term in a contract purports to restrict liability to a specified sum of money, and the question arises for the purposes of this Part of this Act whether it was fair and reasonable to incorporate the term in the contract, then, without prejudice to subsection (2) above, regard shall be had in particular to—
  (a) the resources which the party seeking to rely on that term could expect to be available to him for the purpose of meeting the liability should it arise;

(b) how far it was open to that party to cover himself by insurance.

(4) The onus of proving that it was fair and reasonable to incorporate a term in a contract shall lie on the party so contending.

25.—(1) In this Part of this Act—

"breach of duty" means the breach—

(a) of any obligation, arising from the express or implied terms of a contract, to take reasonable care or exercise reasonable skill in the performance of the contract;

(b) of any common law duty to take reasonable care or exercise reasonable skill;

(c) of the duty of reasonable care imposed by section 2(1) of the Occupiers' Liability (Scotland) Act 1960;

"business" includes a profession and the activities of any government department or local or public authority;

"consumer" has the meaning assigned to that expression in the definition in this section of "consumer contract";

"consumer contract" means a contract (not being a contract of sale by auction or competitive tender) in which—

(a) one party to the contract deals, and the other party to the contract ("the consumer") does not deal or hold himself out as dealing, in the course of a business, and

(b) in the case of a contract such as is mentioned in section 15(2)(a) of this Act, the goods are of a type ordinarily supplied for private use or consumption;

and for the purposes of this Part of this Act the onus of proving that a contract is not to be regarded as a consumer contract shall lie on the party so contending;

"goods" has the same meaning as in the Sale of Goods Act 1893;

"hire-purchase agreement" has the same meaning as in section 189(1) of the Consumer Credit Act 1974;

"personal injury" includes any disease and any impairment of physical or mental condition.

(2) In relation to any breach of duty or obligation, it is immaterial for any purpose of this Part of this Act whether the act or omission giving rise to that breach was inadvertent or

PART II

Interpretation of Part II.

1960 c. 30.

56 & 57 Vict. c. 71.

1974 c. 39.

PART II intentional, or whether liability for it arises directly or vicariously.

(3) In this Part of this Act, any reference to excluding or restricting any liability includes—
  (a) making the liability or its enforcement subject to any restrictive or onerous conditions;
  (b) excluding or restricting any right or remedy in respect of the liability, or subjecting a person to any prejudice in consequence of his pursuing any such right or remedy;
  (c) excluding or restricting any rule of evidence or procedure;
  (d) excluding or restricting any liability by reference to a notice having contractual effect,

but does not include an agreement to submit any question to arbitration.

(4) In subsection (3)(d) above " notice " includes an announcement, whether or not in writing, and any other communication or pretended communication.

(5) In sections 15 and 16 and 19 to 21 of this Act, any reference to excluding or restricting liability for breach of an obligation or duty shall include a reference to excluding or restricting the obligation or duty itself.

PART III

PROVISIONS APPLYING TO WHOLE OF UNITED KINGDOM

Miscellaneous

International supply contracts.
26.—(1) The limits imposed by this Act on the extent to which a person may exclude or restrict liability by reference to a contract term do not apply to liability arising under such a contract as is described in subsection (3) below.

(2) The terms of such a contract are not subject to any requirement of reasonableness under section 3 or 4: and nothing in Part II of this Act shall require the incorporation of the terms of such a contract to be fair and reasonable for them to have effect.

(3) Subject to subsection (4), that description of contract is one whose characteristics are the following—
  (a) either it is a contract of sale of goods or it is one under or in pursuance of which the possession or ownership of goods passes; and

(b) it is made by parties whose places of business (or, if they have none, habitual residences) are in the territories of different States (the Channel Islands and the Isle of Man being treated for this purpose as different States from the United Kingdom).

PART III

(4) A contract falls within subsection (3) above only if either—
   (a) the goods in question are, at the time of the conclusion of the contract, in the course of carriage, or will be carried, from the territory of one State to the territory of another ; or
   (b) the acts constituting the offer and acceptance have been done in the territories of different States ; or
   (c) the contract provides for the goods to be delivered to the territory of a State other than that within whose territory those acts were done.

27.—(1) Where the proper law of a contract is the law of any part of the United Kingdom only by choice of the parties (and apart from that choice would be the law of some country outside the United Kingdom) sections 2 to 7 and 16 to 21 of this Act do not operate as part of the proper law.

Choice of law clauses.

(2) This Act has effect notwithstanding any contract term which applies or purports to apply the law of some country outside the United Kingdom, where (either or both)—
   (a) the term appears to the court, or arbitrator or arbiter to have been imposed wholly or mainly for the purpose of enabling the party imposing it to evade the operation of this Act ; or
   (b) in the making of the contract one of the parties dealt as consumer, and he was then habitually resident in the United Kingdom, and the essential steps necessary for the making of the contract were taken there, whether by him or by others on his behalf.

(3) In the application of subsection (2) above to Scotland, for paragraph (b) there shall be substituted—
   " (b) the contract is a consumer contract as defined in Part II of this Act, and the consumer at the date when the contract was made was habitually resident in the United Kingdom, and the essential steps necessary for the making of the contract were taken there, whether by him or by others on his behalf.".

28.—(1) This section applies to a contract for carriage by sea of a passenger or of a passenger and his luggage where the provisions of the Athens Convention (with or without modification) do not have, in relation to the contract, the force of law in the United Kingdom.

Temporary provision for sea carriage of passengers.

PART III

(2) In a case where—

(a) the contract is not made in the United Kingdom, and

(b) neither the place of departure nor the place of destination under it is in the United Kingdom,

a person is not precluded by this Act from excluding or restricting liability for loss or damage, being loss or damage for which the provisions of the Convention would, if they had the force of law in relation to the contract, impose liability on him.

(3) In any other case, a person is not precluded by this Act from excluding or restricting liability for that loss or damage—

(a) in so far as the exclusion or restriction would have been effective in that case had the provisions of the Convention had the force of law in relation to the contract; or

(b) in such circumstances and to such extent as may be prescribed, by reference to a prescribed term of the contract.

(4) For the purposes of subsection (3)(a), the values which shall be taken to be the official values in the United Kingdom of the amounts (expressed in gold francs) by reference to which liability under the provisions of the Convention is limited shall be such amounts in sterling as the Secretary of State may from time to time by order made by statutory instrument specify.

(5) In this section,—

(a) the references to excluding or restricting liability include doing any of those things in relation to the liability which are mentioned in section 13 or section 25(3) and (5); and

(b) " the Athens Convention " means the Athens Convention relating to the Carriage of Passengers and their Luggage by Sea, 1974; and

(c) " prescribed " means prescribed by the Secretary of State by regulations made by statutory instrument;

and a statutory instrument containing the regulations shall be subject to annulment in pursuance of a resolution of either House of Parliament.

Saving for other relevant legislation.

29.—(1) Nothing in this Act removes or restricts the effect of, or prevents reliance upon, any contractual provision which—

(a) is authorised or required by the express terms or necessary implication of an enactment; or

(b) being made with a view to compliance with an international agreement to which the United Kingdom is a party, does not operate more restrictively than is contemplated by the agreement.

(2) A contract term is to be taken—

(a) for the purposes of Part I of this Act, as satisfying the requirement of reasonableness; and

(b) for those of Part II, to have been fair and reasonable to incorporate,

if it is incorporated or approved by, or incorporated pursuant to a decision or ruling of, a competent authority acting in the exercise of any statutory jurisdiction or function and is not a term in a contract to which the competent authority is itself a party.

(3) In this section—

"competent authority" means any court, arbitrator or arbiter, government department or public authority;

"enactment" means any legislation (including subordinate legislation) of the United Kingdom or Northern Ireland and any instrument having effect by virtue of such legislation; and

"statutory" means conferred by an enactment.

30.—(1) In section 3 of the Consumer Protection Act 1961 (provisions against marketing goods which do not comply with safety requirements), after subsection (1) there is inserted—

"(1A) Any term of an agreement which purports to exclude or restrict, or has the effect of excluding or restricting, any obligation imposed by or by virtue of that section, or any liability for breach of such an obligation, shall be void.".

(2) The same amendment is made in section 3 of the Consumer Protection Act (Northern Ireland) 1965.

Obligations under Consumer Protection Acts.
1961 c. 40.
1965 c. 14 (N.I.).

General

31.—(1) This Act comes into force on 1st February 1978.

(2) Nothing in this Act applies to contracts made before the date on which it comes into force; but subject to this, it applies to liability for any loss or damage which is suffered on or after that date.

(3) The enactments specified in Schedule 3 to this Act are amended as there shown.

(4) The enactments specified in Schedule 4 to this Act are repealed to the extent specified in column 3 of that Schedule.

Commencement; amendments; repeals.

PART III
Citation and extent.

32.—(1) This Act may be cited as the Unfair Contract Terms Act 1977.

(2) Part I of this Act extends to England and Wales and to Northern Ireland; but it does not extend to Scotland.

(3) Part II of this Act extends to Scotland only.

(4) This Part of this Act extends to the whole of the United Kingdom.

SCHEDULES

SCHEDULE 1

Section 1(2).

SCOPE OF SECTIONS 2 TO 4 AND 7

1. Sections 2 to 4 of this Act do not extend to—
    (a) any contract of insurance (including a contract to pay an annuity on human life);
    (b) any contract so far as it relates to the creation or transfer of an interest in land, or to the termination of such an interest, whether by extinction, merger, surrender, forfeiture or otherwise;
    (c) any contract so far as it relates to the creation or transfer of a right or interest in any patent, trade mark, copyright, registered design, technical or commercial information or other intellectual property, or relates to the termination of any such right or interest;
    (d) any contract so far as it relates—
        (i) to the formation or dissolution of a company (which means any body corporate or unincorporated association and includes a partnership), or
        (ii) to its constitution or the rights or obligations of its corporators or members;
    (e) any contract so far as it relates to the creation or transfer of securities or of any right or interest in securities.

2. Section 2(1) extends to—
    (a) any contract of marine salvage or towage;
    (b) any charterparty of a ship or hovercraft; and
    (c) any contract for the carriage of goods by ship or hovercraft;
but subject to this sections 2 to 4 and 7 do not extend to any such contract except in favour of a person dealing as consumer.

3. Where goods are carried by ship or hovercraft in pursuance of a contract which either—
    (a) specifies that as the means of carriage over part of the journey to be covered, or
    (b) makes no provision as to the means of carriage and does not exclude that means,
then sections 2(2), 3 and 4 do not, except in favour of a person dealing as consumer, extend to the contract as it operates for and in relation to the carriage of the goods by that means.

4. Section 2(1) and (2) do not extend to a contract of employment, except in favour of the employee.

5. Section 2(1) does not affect the validity of any discharge and indemnity given by a person, on or in connection with an award to him of compensation for pneumoconiosis attributable to employment in the coal industry, in respect of any further claim arising from his contracting that disease.

Sections 11(2) and 24(2).

SCHEDULE 2

"Guidelines" for Application of Reasonableness Test

The matters to which regard is to be had in particular for the purposes of sections 6(3), 7(3) and (4), 20 and 21 are any of the following which appear to be relevant—

(a) the strength of the bargaining positions of the parties relative to each other, taking into account (among other things) alternative means by which the customer's requirements could have been met;

(b) whether the customer received an inducement to agree to the term, or in accepting it had an opportunity of entering into a similar contract with other persons, but without having to accept a similar term;

(c) whether the customer knew or ought reasonably to have known of the existence and extent of the term (having regard, among other things, to any custom of the trade and any previous course of dealing between the parties);

(d) where the term excludes or restricts any relevant liability if some condition is not complied with, whether it was reasonable at the time of the contract to expect that compliance with that condition would be practicable;

(e) whether the goods were manufactured, processed or adapted to the special order of the customer.

Section 31(3).

SCHEDULE 3

Amendment of Enactments

56 & 57 Vict. c. 71.

In the Sale of Goods Act 1893—

(a) in section 55(1), for the words "the following provisions of this section" substitute "the provisions of the Unfair Contract Terms Act 1977";

(b) in section 62(1), in the definition of "business", for "local authority or statutory undertaker" substitute "or local or public authority".

1973 c. 13.
1974 c. 39.

In the Supply of Goods (Implied Terms) Act 1973 (as originally enacted and as substituted by the Consumer Credit Act 1974)—

(a) in section 14(1) for the words from "conditional sale" to the end substitute "a conditional sale agreement where the buyer deals as consumer within Part I of the Unfair Contract Terms Act 1977 or, in Scotland, the agreement is a consumer contract within Part II of that Act";

(b) in section 15(1), in the definition of "business", for "local authority or statutory undertaker" substitute "or local or public authority".

SCHEDULE 4

Section 31(4).

REPEALS

Chapter	Short title	Extent of repeal
56 & 57 Vict. c. 71.	Sale of Goods Act 1893.	In section 55, subsections (3) to (11). Section 55A. Section 61(6). In section 62(1) the definition of "contract for the international sale of goods".
1962 c. 46.	Transport Act 1962.	Section 43(7).
1967 c. 45.	Uniform Laws on International Sales Act 1967.	In section 1(4), the words "55 and 55A".
1972 c. 33.	Carriage by Railway Act 1972.	In section 1(1), the words from "and shall have" onwards.
1973 c. 13.	Supply of Goods (Implied Terms) Act 1973.	Section 5(1). Section 6. In section 7(1), the words from "contract for the international sale of goods" onwards. In section 12, subsections (2) to (9). Section 13. In section 15(1), the definition of "consumer sale".

The repeals in sections 12 and 15 of the Supply of Goods (Implied Terms) Act 1973 shall have effect in relation to those sections as originally enacted and as substituted by the Consumer Credit Act 1974.

1974 c. 39.

HMSO publications are available from:

HMSO Publications Centre
(Mail and telephone orders only)
PO Box 276, London SW8 5DT
Telephone orders 071-873 9090
General enquiries 071-873 0011
(queuing system in operation for both numbers)
Fax orders 071-873 8200

HMSO Bookshops
49 High Holborn, London, WC1V 6HB
071-873 0011 Fax 071-873 8200 (counter service only)
258 Broad Street, Birmingham, B1 2HE
021-643 3740 Fax 021-643 6510
Southey House, 33 Wine Street, Bristol, BS1 2BQ
0272 264306 Fax 0272 294515
9-21 Princess Street, Manchester, M60 8AS
061-834 7201 Fax 061-833 0634
16 Arthur Street, Belfast, BT1 4GD
0232 238451 Fax 0232 235401
71 Lothian Road, Edinburgh, EH3 9AZ
031-228 4181 Fax 031-229 2734

HMSO's Accredited Agents
(see Yellow Pages)

and through good booksellers

LONDON: HMSO

£4.15 net

ISBN 0-10-545077-4

Unfair Contract Terms Act 1977

1977 CHAPTER 50

ARRANGEMENT OF SECTIONS

PART I

AMENDMENT OF LAW FOR ENGLAND AND WALES AND NORTHERN IRELAND

Introductory

Section
1. Scope of Part I.

Avoidance of liability for negligence, breach of contract, etc.
2. Negligence liability.
3. Liability arising in contract.
4. Unreasonable indemnity clauses.

Liability arising from sale or supply of goods
5. "Guarantee" of consumer goods.
6. Sale and hire-purchase.
7. Miscellaneous contracts under which goods pass.

Other provisions about contracts
8. Misrepresentation.
9. Effect of breach.
10. Evasion by means of secondary contract.

Explanatory provisions
11. The "reasonableness" test.
12. "Dealing as consumer".
13. Varieties of exemption clause.
14. Interpretation of Part I.

PART II

AMENDMENT OF LAW FOR SCOTLAND

15. Scope of Part II.
16. Liability for breach of duty.
17. Control of unreasonable exemptions in consumer or standard form contracts.

A

Section
18. Unreasonable indemnity clauses in consumer contracts.
19. " Guarantee " of consumer goods.
20. Obligations implied by law in sale and hire-purchase contracts.
21. Obligations implied by law in other contracts for the supply of goods.
22. Consequence of breach.
23. Evasion by means of secondary contract.
24. The " reasonableness " test.
25. Interpretation of Part II.

PART III

PROVISIONS APPLYING TO WHOLE OF UNITED KINGDOM

Miscellaneous

26. International supply contracts.
27. Choice of law clauses.
28. Temporary provision for sea carriage of passengers.
29. Saving for other relevant legislation.
30. Obligations under Consumer Protection Acts.

General

31. Commencement; amendments; repeals.
32. Citation and extent.

SCHEDULES:

Schedule 1—Scope of ss. 2 to 4 and 7.
Schedule 2—" Guidelines " for application of reasonableness test.
Schedule 3—Amendment of enactments.
Schedule 4—Repeals.